The Adventur

and Stormie

GW01403237

Pam Piecha

Copyright © 2024

All rights reserved.

ISBN:979-8-89122-362-2

Dedication

I dedicate this book to my mother, who read to us nightly when we were kids and gave me a love of reading.

To my husband, Rich, who encouraged me to write this book.

To my son Josh, who inspired these stories and Stormie, who was the best dog ever.

To all my English teachers who taught me the importance of writing down our ideas and doing it using proper English and grammar.

Table of Contents

About the Author

Pamela is the eldest of 5 children and grew up on the Northwest side of Chicago. Her mother fostered a love of reading by gathering all 5 of her children around her for story time. Her mom taught her how to read at the age of 4, and her love of books began. While on vacation, Pamela would even take a row boat out alone with a good book. She shared her love of books with her youngest sister by taking her to the library. Pamela grew up to teach young children in her church's Awana program for several years. She has a love for family and the Lord. She has been married to her husband, Rich, for over 30 years. She has wanted to write a book about her son, Josh, and has worked on it for a couple of years. This book is the product of that hard work. As a first-time author, she just wants to write stories for those who love to read to children.

Page Left Blank Intentionally

They Meet

This is Stormie. Stormie is a happy dog. He's happy because he lives in a shelter, and today's the day families come in to adopt the pets who live here.

This is Josh. He is 6 years old. Josh is excited today because this is the day his parents promised to take him to the shelter to adopt a dog.

Josh and his parents arrive at the shelter and start their search for the perfect dog. Josh looks around at all the choices and sees Stormie off in a corner. Stormie sees Josh as well and starts to wag his tail.

Stormie runs over to meet Josh. It was the start of a wonderful friendship. Josh and his parents adopt Stormie and bring him home. That's when the adventures begin.

First, they go out in the yard and play with a ball. Josh teaches Stormie how to play fetch and some other tricks, like sitting, staying, and rolling over.

Josh loves to take Stormie for walks around his neighborhood. He introduces him to all his friends.

They go to the park and watch a baseball game. Stormie starts to chase the ball and the players must stop him so they can continue playing.

Josh's grandparents come over to meet Stormie, and he kisses them and lets them scratch his ears. They tell Josh that Stormie is a good choice.

The next day, Josh must go to school, and his mom lets Stormie ride with them. When they get to school, Josh shows Stormie to all his classmates. They all love him and are sad when they must go inside.

After school, Josh takes Stormie for another walk, and they meet other dogs. All the dogs get along and play with each other.

Josh continues to teach Stormie other tricks. He learns how to sit and shake paws, and he learns to speak when you ask him to. He expects treats after each trick.

At night, Stormie wants to sleep with Josh, but we don't let him do it because he has his bed.

Josh and Stormie go for a Walk

Today, Josh is going to take Stormie for a walk around the neighborhood. It's a beautiful sunny day.

The first person they meet is the mail carrier. He has a package for Josh. It is a box full of dog toys for Stormie. One of the things in there is a frisbee. They decide to take that with them on their walk.

The next person they meet is Billy and his dog Coco. They all want to play with the Frisbee. The boys take turns throwing it to their dogs, and the dogs have lots of fun trying to catch it.

Now, it's time to continue their walk. As they walk, Stormie spots a cute little bunny. He wants to try and play with it. The bunny lets Stormie sniff her and even jumps around so he can chase her a little. Stormie doesn't want to hurt her; he just wants to be friends.

They continue their journey, and now they see Josh's friend Betty. Betty doesn't have a pet of her own, so she loves to pet Stormie. Josh and Betty talk for a while and Stormie rests in the grass.

Soon, it's time to move on. Now they see Mr. Benson. He loves to play fetch with Stormie, so he gets a ball and tosses it. Stormie runs and brings it back. This goes on for a few minutes until Stormie looks a little thirsty. Josh brings some water and gives him a drink.

As they continue they meet up with Mrs. Smith. She has a cat named Shadow. Shadow and Stormie don't always get along, so Josh just tells her about his day. Before they leave, she gives Stormie a treat.

It's starting to get late, and it's almost lunchtime, so they start to head home. Josh's mommy asks how the walk was, and Josh tells her all about the people and animals they met today.

I wonder what they will do tomorrow.

Josh and Stormie go to the Zoo

When Josh wakes up today, he notices that it is a beautiful sunny day. So, he asks his parents if they could go to the zoo, and since they don't have to work today, they agree. Now, Josh lives in a city where they let pets in as long as they behave. His parents make sandwiches and pack snacks, and off they go.

When they arrive, they talk about which animals to see first and decide on the lions. The lion is sleeping, and

Josh seems disappointed until his dad explains that lions sleep most of the day and maybe they will be awake later. Stormie seems to like them.

Then, they see the tigers and leopards. Their cubs are all out playing, and it makes Josh laugh. Stormie is really interested in watching them play.

As they walk, they notice some geese lying in the grass. Josh has to really hold Stormie back since he wants to play with them. Most geese don't like to play.

Now, they go to see Josh's favorite animal, the dolphin. They are training at the time, and Josh gets to see them do many tricks. They jump through hoops and hit a ball into a basket. Stormie wants to chase the ball, too.

The next animal they went to see was his mom's favorite, the polar bear. The polar bears could be seen through a giant glass window. They were swimming, and Stormie really liked watching them. It must have reminded him of his pool.

They all got a little hungry and found a picnic table to set up lunch. They enjoy their sandwiches and snacks. Even Stormie has some food.

Oh boy, now Dad is excited because they are going to see his favorite animal, the wolves. They know Stormie is going to love them, and he does. They look a lot like him. He thought he was going to be able to play with them and seemed sad that he couldn't.

They continue to see the monkeys and gorillas. Those are lots of fun to watch. They are all playing with each other, and the mamas are holding their babies.

It is now time to go home, but they need to stop by the lion one more time on the way out. The lion is awake and even lets out a big roar when he sees Stormie.

On the ride home, they talk about all they have seen until Josh and Stormie both fall asleep. All in all, it was a great day.

Josh and Stormie Celebrate Josh's Birthday

Today is Josh's birthday, and they are having a big party with lots of guests. Even Stormie seems excited as they set up and decorate. He could tell something big was happening.

The guests are starting to arrive, and then things get fun. Josh's grandparents are the first to arrive. They give him a new bicycle. Wow, Josh is excited about that one.

Then it is his Uncle Chris, Aunt Gloria, and cousin Chris. They give him a guitar, and Uncle Chris even shows him how to play it a little. He will probably need lessons.

After them are his Auntie Deb and Uncle Marty. They also bring his cousins Kyle, Kelly, Kaylee, and Kolby. Their gift is a basketball hoop. This family loves to play basketball and even taught Josh some trick shots.

Auntie Tray, Uncle Dave, and cousin Audrey are the next to arrive. They give him some great books to read. Auntie Tray is a teacher and knows the importance of reading.

The next ones to arrive are Uncle Mike, Auntie Jeanette, and their children. They gave Josh a race track. Stormie wants to chase the cars around the track. That makes everyone laugh.

Josh's Uncle Lou, Auntie Susana, and all their kids are next. They give Josh a baseball mitt and bat. That makes Stormie excited since he loves to chase the baseballs.

It is now time to sing Happy Birthday and eat the cake. Everyone enjoyed the day, and they all left happy.

Stormie and Josh spend the rest of the night playing with all the new gifts. They end the day with Josh reading a book to Stormie.

It was the best birthday ever.

Josh and Stormie Visit a Farm

Josh's parents have a surprise for them today. They are going to visit a farm, and this is going to be a lot of fun. They pack up their car with some snacks and water for the long ride. Stormie sits and looks out the window at the changing scenery. Josh notices that there are fewer and fewer buildings and more and more fields.

After a couple of hours, they arrive at the farm. The farmer and his wife are friends of Josh's parents and greet them enthusiastically. They are happy to see Josh and Stormie and are excited to show them around the farm.

They tell Josh that Stormie must stay on his leash as they go around the farm. The first place they go is the chicken coop. The farmer shows Josh how to look for and gather eggs. They are able to gather 10 eggs, and the farmer's wife says she will save them for Josh to take home with him.

The next place they go is to the barn where the cows are kept. Stormie seems a little afraid of the cows because they are so large. He stays back at the door with Josh's dad. The farmer shows Josh how to milk one of the cows. Josh really likes doing that and has a lot of fun.

There is a small lake on the property, and the farmer's wife has planned a picnic near it. They can swim and play in the water. They allow Stormie to be off his leash so he can play with Josh. They eat a great meal of sandwiches, potato salad, and freshly baked brownies. It is all delicious.

Now, they are off to see some of the other animals on the farm. Josh puts Stormie's leash back on so he doesn't get frightened by the other animals. The farmer takes them to a field where the sheep are grazing and eating grass. He says it's time for them to come back to their pen closer to the barn. Stormie gets very excited when he sees the sheep because he is the kind of dog that usually works guiding sheep back to their pen. The farmer has a dog that does that for him, but he lets Stormie try to do it as well. Stormie does a great job, and all the sheep are back in their pens. Now Stormie must have his leash put back on again.

The farmer has a special surprise for Josh. He is going to take him for a ride on an ATV, an all-terrain vehicle. They leave Stormie and Josh's parents to rest in the shade while Josh gets to tour the rest of the property. He sees some of the crops the farmer is growing.

When they return, Josh's dad says that it is time to go home. They are all a little tired and agree to leave. The farmer and his wife pack up the eggs that Josh gathered, as well as some of the brownies that were left.

They say their goodbyes and head home. Josh is still too excited and wants to talk about all the great things they did and saw. Stormie is happy to just look out the window as they drive home. It was another wonderful day. I can't wait to see what they do next.

Josh and Stormie go to a Baseball Game

Josh woke up very excited today. His parents found out that the local baseball team was having a dog day at the stadium. They were able to get tickets for the whole family and Stormie is coming with them.

The game is in the afternoon, so they have time to prepare. Josh packs his baseball mitt and some bowls for Stormie's water.

When they get to the stadium, they find they have great seats right near the players' seats. They may even be able to meet some of them.

The first thing they do is introduce Stormie to some of the other dogs near them. All the dogs get along and sniff each other. They all seem to like each other, and none of them fight.

There is still time before the game starts and some of the players are signing balls and giving them to the children as souvenirs. Josh met a few of the players and got two balls to take home. One of the players signs Josh's cap.

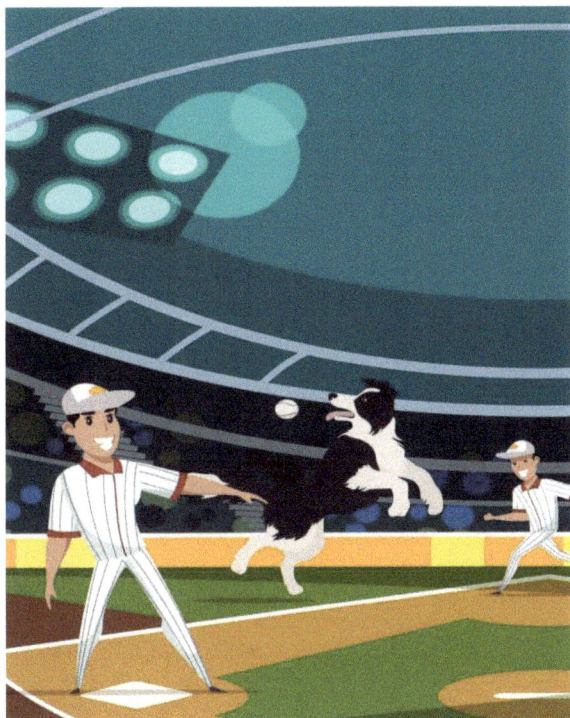

His dad goes and gets some hot dogs for all of them.
Even Stormie is getting one. They are so yummy. He also
gets drinks for Josh and his mom. He even gets some water
for Stormie. Later, he treats them to ice cream sundaes in
small plastic baseball caps. They even have pup cups for
the dogs, which are just plain vanilla ice cream.

Now, it's almost time for the game to begin, so
everyone takes their seats so that they can watch the
game. The team takes the field, and all the dogs get
excited to see the baseballs. One of them tries to get on the

field to chase them, but its owner stops him. Now that everyone is settled down, the game can begin.

The home team scores first in the 2nd inning, and the visiting team scores in the 3rd inning. It's a tied game now and stays that way until the bottom of the 9th inning when the home team scores again and wins the game.

The announcer then says he has a surprise for all the children and dogs. They are all going to be able to run the bases with the team. Josh and Stormie wait their turn and have a great time running the bases with the others.

It was a great time, and Josh and Stormie both fell asleep on the way home. There are many more stories to come about their adventures. But for now, it's the end until next time.